Name

Happy Birthday!

*P.S. There are
several stories
by Bill.*

The IT Book

Also by Kathie Gedden

Beginning Piano: The Way I Teach It

(www.amazon.com)

MY FATHER - Coming 2012

(www.amazon.com)

The IT Book

Short Stories of Encouragement for Children of All Ages

KATHIE GEDDEN

Inspiring Voices®
A Service of **Guideposts**

Inspiring Voices books may be ordered through booksellers or by contacting:

Inspiring Voices
1663 Liberty Drive
Bloomington, IN 47403
www.inspiringvoices.com
1-(866) 697-5313

Because of the dynamic nature of the Internet, any web addresses or links contained in this book may have changed since publication and may no longer be valid. The views expressed in this work are solely those of the author and do not necessarily reflect the views of the publisher, and the publisher hereby disclaims any responsibility for them.

Certain stock imagery © Thinkstock.
Any people depicted in stock imagery provided by Thinkstock are models, and such images are being used for illustrative purposes only.

ISBN: 978-1-4624-0006-5 (e)
ISBN: 978-1-4624-0005-8 (sc)

Library of Congress Control Number: 2011937277

Printed in the United States of America

Inspiring Voices rev. date: 9/28/2011

To my mother, Katherine Flynn Gedden,
who often encouraged me to write, and who
could well have been a writer herself.

To my husband, Bill Mercer,
the joy and encourager of my life.

ACKNOWLEDGMENTS

Special thanks to my friend,

Jessica Krakow,

for editing my book and

for her invaluable suggestions.

TABLE OF CONTENTS

LISTEN TO IT

Once upon a time there was a little boy who didn't like to go to school. He thought that school was hard. He wanted to stay outside and play. He didn't understand why people go to school. He thought school was boring.

One day when he was sitting on a bench at recess, a friend of his came and sat down next to him. This little boy enjoyed school. He loved to learn new things. He liked to do new things. He felt sorry that his friend dreaded going to school. He decided to tell him his secret game, a game he made up in his own mind. This game was the reason he liked school.

Here is the secret game that he shared with his friend. This is a different kind of a game. It is different because he played this game with himself. Every morning before school started, he remembered his game. He began playing his game the very moment that the teacher began to talk. His game was a challenge to himself. He challenged himself to listen to every word that the teacher said all day. He tried never to miss a single word that the teacher said. He played this game all day every school day. Then an amazing thing happened. His game started getting easier. He started enjoying it more and more, and doing his homework started getting easier and easier because he knew so many of the answers. He had learned them during the day playing his listening game. Then he realized that he was learning lots of new and interesting things every day by listening.

He was excited about going to school, about learning to read, about all the new people and places he would learn about when he could read books. He looked forward to all the things he could learn to do, and to make, and to explore.

He began to think that the world is a place of wonder, and that every day could be a challenge to learn more. He knew that he had learned to love to learn.

Listening was his secret game.

The other little boy who thought school was boring watched his friend and began to listen.

LISTEN TO IT

PICTURE IT

A little girl moved with her family to a house right next door to a golf course. She was glad because she wanted to learn to play golf. Her father bought her a set of golf clubs, just the right size for her. She went with her father, then with her brother, then with her friends to play golf. But she never could hit the ball into the hole. She watched other people playing golf. They always hit the ball into the hole at least some of the time. She wondered why she couldn't seem to do it.

One day she went to the golf course with her mother. Her mother said, "Try putting the ball just a few inches from the hole. Take a good look at that hole, then at the ball. Then close your eyes and picture that ball and that hole in your mind. Then in your mind see yourself slowly hitting that ball into that hole. Keep picturing that in your mind many times until tomorrow. Tomorrow we will come back and try again."

Tomorrow came and the little girl and her mother returned to the golf course. The little girl had faithfully, calmly pictured herself hitting the ball into the hole. She placed the ball in the same place where she had put it the day before. Then, still concentrating on the ball and the hole, she slowly hit the ball and it went into the hole. Nearly every time that she concentrated, the ball went into the hole.

Each time that she went to the golf course, she placed the ball a little farther away from the hole. She pictured this not only when she was at the golf course but many times throughout the day.

She started really enjoying picturing herself successfully, slowly hitting the ball into the hole.

As the weeks and months went by, she became better and better. She had learned the secret of success.

PICTURE IT

LOVE IT

Once upon a time there was a little boy who felt very sad. He didn't have any brothers or sisters. His parents worked late at night, so a babysitter stayed with him until they came home. When his parents were not at home, he wasn't allowed to have friends over. He felt very sorry for himself.

But one night his parents brought a surprise home for him. It was a little dog, a real dog. He could hardly believe his eyes. His father told him that if he would take very good care of the puppy, that he could give him a name and keep him and it could be his very own dog.

His parents showed him how to feed the dog, and give it water, and brush it and pet it, how to take it out into the backyard and run and play with it.

The little boy named his dog Zeke. He took very good care of him. They became good friends. The little dog loved him.

One day the little boy realized that he was no longer sad. He was happy. He had someone to love, a friend, a little dog.

LOVE IT

TREASURE IT

When I was a little girl, some of my favorite times were spent with my grandmother. Everything about her and her home made me happy.

She was the organist at our church where my father was the choir director. She poured out her love for God at both the organ and the piano.

Her home was lovely, and she dressed so nicely in her pretty dresses and shoes and hats and gloves. Her big yard was a fairyland to me. I knew every inch of it, all the flowers, bushes, tall trees. I made little tea sets out of fallen acorns.

I loved to stay overnight with my grandmother and sleep in her big bed upstairs with her. I liked to listen to the wind in the tall trees.

One day my Nana took me downstairs to a big cabinet full of books. She reached in and took out the book <u>HEIDI</u> and handed it to me for my very own. It is still one of my favorite stories.

She drove me in her little car and we went many places around town together. We liked to go for walks together too.

I remember so many things that we did together, but I do not remember much that she said. She was a gentle, rather quiet person and whenever she said something, it was always kind.

But one thing that she said over and over, I will never forget. Every single time someone asked her how she was, she answered: "Just fine, thank you."

Do you know someone who was a joy and an inspiration to you like my Nana was to me?

TREASURE IT

SPEAK IT

Speaking positive thoughts can make our day.

When we were children, we almost wore out the record, "The Little Engine That Could." We listened to it so often. Those words the little engine spoke have stayed with me all my life. "I think I can. I think I can. I think I can. I know I can. I know I can. I know I can. I knew I could."

Speaking positive thoughts can make the day for others too.

Perhaps the most comforting, encouraging words ever spoken are "I'm sorry." Perhaps the most comforting words ever thought and felt are "I forgive you."

We never know how much a kind word will mean to those we meet during the day: at the grocery checkout, at the Post Office, on the phone with someone taking an order, to a waitress at a restaurant, to anyone performing a service for us, to name a few.

Some people are astounded to hear a kind word spoken to them.

It takes so little effort and gives such joy to the giver and the receiver.

SPEAK IT

ENJOY IT

the Sun

the sky

the clouds

the stars

a flower

a rose

a tulip

a sunflower

a violet

wildflowers

a bird

a bird song

a tree

an acorn

a leaf turning color

a blade of grass

a hill

a valley

a bike ride

a hike

a mountain

a path

a stream

a river

a lake

a pond

an ocean

a seashell

a rock

a swim

a vegetable garden

an ear of corn

a vine-ripened tomato

a cucumber

a fruit tree

an apple

a peach

an orange

an evergreen tree

pine cones

a nut tree

pecans

walnuts

a butterfly

a patch of shade

a breeze

a breath of fresh air

the wind whistling

a baby deer

a raindrop

a rainbow

a castle in the sand

a ride on a swing

a peaceful summer afternoon

a hammock

a book

a picnic

a watermelon

a firefly

a windmill

a farm

a pony

a sleigh ride

a snowflake

a snowman

I enjoy discovering new favorite things. What things do you enjoy?

ENJOY IT

TRY IT

Is there anything you can think of that you wanted to try to do but just never did it? Maybe there are several things.

Think back as far as you can to your childhood. One summer day when my brothers and sister and I were growing up we tried very hard to accomplish something. Our parents had driven us to one of my favorite places, The Ledges State Park. There were very high hills to climb and valleys with streams running through them. We spent all day hiking. As we walked along we noticed a little dog following us. He was so hungry. He was just skin and bones. All day he followed us and all day we begged to take him home with us. All day the answer was no. As we were driving up those hills to leave the park, the little dog followed us. The little dog had no collar and desperately needed a home. We begged and begged and finally our Dad said yes. We called him Skippy. That was the beginning of my Dad's love affair with dogs.

If there is anything you want to accomplish

TRY IT

TEACH IT

I am a piano teacher. For twenty-five years I have gone to people's homes to teach them.

I have made many friends, not only my students but also their families, and I've had many wonderful experiences. Here is a priceless one.

For about a year I had been teaching a little girl. We'll say her name is Karen. One afternoon after her lesson, Karen stepped out of the room. Her father who had been sitting in the room, walked over to the piano, sat down and began to play.

I said, "I didn't know you could play the piano!" And he said, "Every week after my daughter finished her lesson, she taught me everything she learned. So now I can play too."

Is there something you have learned or something you could learn that you could teach?

Maybe you are in kindergarten or first grade and are learning the alphabet. Do you have younger brothers or sisters or younger neighbor children? Perhaps you could teach them the alphabet. Maybe sing the alphabet song over and over with them until they know it. How much easier it will be for them when they start school.

Perhaps you are a little older and have already learned to read. Maybe you have younger brothers or sisters you could read to, or perhaps a grandparent or an elderly neighbor. Remember the joy that Heidi brought to the elderly blind grandmother by reading her favorite hymns to her?

There is no end to the possible things we can learn and teach.

Try learning something new. Then

TEACH IT

LEARN IT

I once knew a person who told me that she tried to learn one new thing every day. What a meaningful way to live, to always be looking for something new.

What are some ways to do this?

READING

The possibilities are endless.

LOOKING

Perhaps you'll find a wildflower or a rock or a bush that you've never noticed before, or a picture on a friend's wall, or a kind of car that you've never noticed, or a kind of butterfly.

Perhaps you could go to a museum or an art gallery or a nature center.

LISTENING

Perhaps you know someone who has lived a lot longer than you have. Perhaps he or she would enjoy telling you how life was different when they were growing up. Maybe they played games or had hobbies or sang songs that are new to you. Maybe they could tell you stories that their parents or grandparents told them.

Or maybe you could sit outside on a nice day and just LISTEN. How many sounds do you hear? Maybe you will hear a birdsong that you've never heard before. Or perhaps you could ask a high school student or college student to teach you one new thing that they are learning.

If you are an older adult, perhaps you could ask your grandchild or neighbor boy or girl to teach you something about computers.

MAKING

Do you knit or crochet or sew? Design something new and make it.

Do you draw or paint? Create a new picture.

Do you like to work with wood or build things? Think of a new project and build it.

Do you like music? Whistle or hum or sing a new tune. Or if you play an instrument, make up a new piece and play it. Have a tape recorder ready so you can record your new song. Maybe in days to come you will think up more new tunes and add them to your tape.

WRITING

Do you like to make up new stories or poems? Write them down in a special notebook. Perhaps you will keep adding to them. Maybe you will find someday that you would enjoy being an author.

If you start adding to this list or making your own list of ways to learn new things, your list will probably grow longer every day.

LEARN IT

GROW IT

One of my most enjoyable activities is working in our little vegetable garden.

I love being out in the sunshine and fresh air, planting (or watching my husband plant), watering, taking leftover vegetable water from steaming vegetables, or egg shells, or coffee grounds and digging them into the ground to nourish the growing plants. But most of all, I enjoy the thrill of seeing those little plants peek up through the ground, and watching them grow a little more each day. What wonder! What joy!

And then after time, sunshine, warm weather, water, and loving care have done their work, the harvest: this year onions, lettuce, green beans and peppers. My husband, Bill, and I think that harvesting those green beans is like an Easter egg hunt. We pick and pick and pick them until we're sure we have them all. But every single time, we spot one or two or even many more that we have missed.

Perhaps you don't have a yard for a garden, but maybe you have a porch on a house, or a little balcony with your apartment. If not, perhaps you have a sunny window sill where you could put a potted plant.

I think if I could grow only one vegetable, it would be a pepper plant, with little peppers. They look like hot chile peppers, but they have a milder taste. We have them in our garden this year. The ones we have start out yellow, then turn orange, then red. They add such bright dashes of color to our garden. The plants are just loaded with peppers, with more and more each week, enough to share with friends.

After we pick them, we wash and dry them and spread them out on the counter. With time they start to wrinkle and get hard. Then we put them in a bowl on the counter. They can be used when soft or hard.

They can be used all year long in cooking, providing a wonderful aroma to the air, a delicious taste to the food, and lots of Vitamin A, Vitamin C and other nutrients.

Just one little chopped up pepper does all that!

GROW IT

GIVE IT

a smile

a kind word

a thank you

a flower

a lovely thought

a prayer

fruit from your fruit trees

vegetables from your garden

cookies you baked

a song

a poem

a hug

a little extra effort

an "extra mile"

a compliment

a surprise

time spent with someone lonely

an "I love you"

words of gratitude

to parents

to children

to friends

to a spouse

an email

a phone call

a visit

a word of encouragement

a pat on the back

a word of praise

time spent doing volunteer work

clothing

food to a food pantry

Anything that will make the world a better place.

GIVE IT

APPRECIATE IT

THIS DAY   APPRECIATE IT

Can you SEE your family, your home, the wonders of nature, flowers, all the lovely things there are to see, the stars, the moon, a sunset? Appreciate it.

Can you HEAR a birdsong, music, your friend's voice, a baby's giggle, all the lovely things there are to hear? Appreciate it.

Can you TASTE the meal prepared by a loved one, the different taste of each food – a banana, a tomato, an onion, a lima bean, a carrot, salt? Appreciate it.

Can you SMELL the fragrance of a rose, the different fragrance of each flower, the aroma of food cooking, of different kinds of spices, of baby's hair? Appreciate it.

Can you TOUCH velvet, peach fuzz, a kitten, water, a friend's hand?

APPRECIATE IT

REMEMBER IT

I remember fondly my years growing up on 36th Street in Des Moines, Iowa.

I remember at age three going with my parents to see the big house for sale that was soon to become our home for over sixty years.

I remember the big living room, dining room, and sunroom, the dark woodwork, the big backyard with a two seated swing in what is now the rock wall.

We moved into that big house with the basement, first floor, second floor, and attic.

I remember the wringer washer in the basement, and my father often helping my mother hang all those diapers and clothes on the clotheslines in the backyard.

I remember the icebox and the ice man carrying the big chunk of ice to put in it to keep the food cold.

I remember the coal room in the basement with a window large enough for the coal man to shovel coal through. I remember my father going down to the basement early every winter morning to shovel coal from the coal room into the stoker so the furnace would have fuel all day long.

I remember the Victory gardens (must have been left from the war days when neighbors each had a little plot of land to grow food) just a block and a half away, where Dahl's supermarket and parking lot is now.

I remember the Flynn dairy horse drawn milk wagon driving up 36th Street.

And I remember that when I was seven in 1949 we got our first car, a brand new green Chevy. I can still see it now. Cars were hard to come by in those years after World War II, but the car dealer admired my Dad and he took that Chevy right off the showroom floor and sold it to him.

After we got the car, I remember my Mother driving us to school every morning and saying as she did every time, "God be with you and have a good day."

Best of all I remember our neighborhood, our neighbors. We were like one huge happy family. People didn't lock their doors in those days. Families had one car only which they parked in their garage or driveway, so there were no cars parked on the street. We had neighborhood ball games constantly in the street, and later on, neighborhood picnics.

The Lewis family next door had a ping pong table in their basement, and Mr. Lewis taught me how to play ping pong with English on it. That means to put a spin on the ball to make it go a different direction. Later we got our own pool table which could be converted into a ping pong table. Endless years of games were enjoyed there by all of us. I am the oldest of six. I have one sister, Mary, and four brothers, Joe, Steve, Paul, and Fred.

I remember the day a man came to our neighborhood with a pony. He went from house to house to take pictures of children, sitting one at a time on the pony dressed like a cowboy or cowgirl. We still have those three pictures of Joe, Mary and myself.

I lived in a busy happy family and neighborhood.

I love to

REMEMBER IT

SING IT

When I was growing up, my life was filled with music. My father was choir director and part time organist at our church. He poured his heart and soul into the choir music. The choir members loved it. At different times, our mother, myself, or other members of our family sang in Dad's choir. And our grandmother was the organist.

Dad and I had grand times at home – Dad at the piano, the two of us singing Christmas carols (in English and in German), Stephen Foster songs, patriotic songs, all kinds of songs.

My mother had a beautiful alto voice. She could harmonize beautifully. She sang lullabies to us and Irish songs.

Our family sang carols together at Christmas.

I loved to sing and my claim to fame was that I sang "Galway Bay" in an eighth grade play.

My father said that when he was growing up, often you could hear his mother or one of his sisters burst into song in another part of the house. He said: "That is the sign of a happy person."

Our Aunt Mary had a beautiful voice and I loved to hear her sing when she came to visit. She taught music and had high school glee clubs that earned superior ratings.

My husband, Bill, loves to sing too. At Christmastime when we drive to see the lights, we sing Christmas carols together. I enjoy it when he sings two of his favorite hymns for me: "How Great Thou Art" and "In the Garden". We sing lots of songs on driving trips.

A friend of mine loves to sing. I play the piano and she sings. Sometimes we sing together. She often says that she feels much better after she sings.

Singing lifts our spirits.

SING IT

EARN IT

My younger sister, Mary, still enjoys reminding me that when she was little, I made her walk around to the neighbors and ask for work. She says that I told her that she was supposed to do the work and then bring the money home to me. But she said that she was smart enough to keep the money herself. However, she does admit that this experience was the start of her working career. Fortunately, I do not remember any of this.

It seemed that when I was in high school, other than going to school and doing homework, by choice, I worked much of the time. I did a lot of babysitting. I worked in a card and pen shop downtown, selling greeting cards and selling and gift wrapping pens. One summer, I worked forty hours a week trying to read and type farmers' signatures for a corn company.

It was a good feeling earning money. My father showed me how to open a savings account so I could watch my money accumulate.

I learned a lot about hard work by watching my father and mother. I don't think they ever stopped working, but they were happy. I used to tease my Mom saying that I don't ever remember her sitting down, except for meals. And she used to tease us by saying: "I just love to watch people work."

I learned that there are different ways of earning:

Earning money

Earning a sense of accomplishment by studying and teaching

Earning a good feeling inside by keeping busy all day long doing whatever needs to be done.

EARN IT

MAIL IT

I heard of a man who was a bed-ridden invalid. Instead of feeling sorry for himself, he wrote and mailed letters, over a thousand a year. He wrote and mailed these letters to other invalids to encourage them and give them joy. These folks wrote back to him and to each other, giving purpose and joy to them all.

Some people write and mail letters of encouragement to our servicemen and women overseas.

Some write thank you letters to parents or children, relatives and friends.

Some people have pen pals. My cousin, Josef, in Germany and I started writing to each other when we were high school age. We kept writing for thirty years until 1984 when he and his son, Christoph, came to visit us. That was 27 years ago and we are still writing only now we email.

Some mail Birthday cards, get well cards or sympathy cards. Some mail a little note to say "I'm thinking of you" to a friend.

There are so many ways to mail a little joy in this world.

MAIL IT

OVERCOME IT

In 1967, our Aunt Katchen and Uncle Willi flew from their home in Dusseldorf, Germany to visit us. Our Dad and Aunt Katchen were brother and sister. Dad came on a big ocean liner to the United States in 1928 when he was 18 years old. He had not seen his sister or any of his large family in all those years. Aunt Katchen wanted so much to see her brother and all of us. She had never been out of Germany, didn't speak a word of English, had never been on a plane and was mortally afraid of flying.

As they were flying across the Atlantic ocean, Uncle Willi noticing how nervous Aunt Katchen was, tried to reassure her. He said "Don't worry. I'll save you." She replied "You can't even swim, you old fool."

Her desire to see her brother overcame her fear.

If there is some fear preventing you from accomplishing something you earnestly want to do

OVERCOME IT

EXPLORE IT

For ten years my husband Bill and I lived in the Colorado mountains. Almost every weekend that weather permitted, we drove and hiked and climbed in Rocky Mountain National Park.

From the Longs Peak area and Lily Lake in the southeast, from Alberta Falls, Bear Lake, Dream Lake, Emerald Lake, Deer Mountain in the northeast, from the Tundra Trail (one of the most awesome places I've ever been) across from the Visitors Center near the top of Trail Ridge Road in the northwest, from Adams Falls and the long trail along the east side of Shadow Mountain Lake near Grand Lake, we explored.

Old Fall River road, the original dirt road with sharp switchbacks, is nine miles long and goes in one direction only, UP. It starts at Endovalley Park (El. 8,558 ft.) and ends at Fall River Pass (El. 11, 796 ft.) near the Alpine Visitors Center.

We enjoyed many hikes partway up the road.

One day just before we started up the mountain, we spotted a large Rocky Mountain bighorn ram on a ledge 15 – 20 feet above us. As we left Endovalley Park and started up the road, we kept an eye out for marmots that live in rocks on a slope above the park.

We reveled in wildflowers along the edge of the road.

About half a mile up we reached Chiquita Creek cascading down the mountain over a succession of falls. We walked over the bridge and on up the road.

If we had ten more years there, we probably could not explore and enjoy all of that awesome Park, all the peaks, the views, all the waterfalls, the trails, mountain wild flowers of countless colors (some as tiny as the head of a pin up at the highest elevations).

This is my most precious memory. One day when I was there alone, just a few steps from me, a newly born tiny deer wobbled and shook on its little legs (maybe taking its first steps).

What parks, monuments, or places of interest could you explore in your state? At a Visitor's Center or online, you may be able to find places that are new to you.

EXPLORE IT

DO IT

Build a kite. Fly it.

Get a book. Read it.

Think an idea. Write about it.

Make a puzzle. Draw a picture. Cut it into pieces of different sizes and shapes. Mix them up. Put the pieces back together again. Make an easy puzzle with big pieces. Make a more difficult puzzle with small pieces.

Set a goal to walk a mile. Do it.

Bake something for a friend. Do it.

What do you want to accomplish? Do it.

Enjoy this day.

DO IT

DAYDREAM IT

Perhaps it's a beautiful place you would like to go to, or a lovely place you once went to, or an imaginary place you could go to in your imagination.

Maybe it's a mountain, or a beach, or a forest. Maybe it's a country farm or a rose garden.

Once we went on a short trip in Colorado through a mountain pass. We stopped at a ranger's station and hiked to the peak of a mountain. Near the top was a huge field of wildflowers. All I have to do is daydream about those flowers to be happy, peaceful, inspired.

Maybe it is Disneyland or Disneyworld.

Maybe it's a ride on a roller coaster or a riverboat or in an airplane.

Wherever, whatever it is, go on a vacation in your mind.

DAYDREAM IT

COLLECT IT

Some people like to collect stamps.

Some people like to collect coins.

Some collect post cards or paintings by their favorite artist.

Some collect books.

Some collect antiques, or dolls, or toys, or recipes.

My husband's mother collected salt and pepper shakers. He said that every time they went on vacation, she would try to find a new and unique set. Then all she had to do was look at her collection to recall those vacations.

Is there something you like to collect?

I like to collect poems or phrases or sentences that are inspiring or helpful. I have a special notebook where

I write these down when I hear or read or come across them.

It's not necessary to collect something, but it can be fun.

COLLECT IT

REACH IT

There are so many meanings for the word **REACH**.
Here are a few of them:

You can reach out your hand to shake someone's hand to wish them "hello" or to congratulate them on achieving something.

My husband, Bill, told me of one little girl's achievement. When he was coaching a group of 6, 7 and 8 year old girls in softball, there was a little girl with some physical problems. She required thick glasses and had a hip problem that made it hard for her to run. When she batted, she couldn't see the ball well and jumped away from every pitch. She was very disappointed about never getting on base. Bill thought that maybe by turning around to bunt so she could look directly at the pitcher, she would be able to see the ball. They tried this in the next game and for the first time she reached first base. He said that her smile was worth all the effort.

You can "reach" across an ocean with a letter or an email.

You can reach the end of the route on a bus or a train.

You can reach the finish line in a race.

You can set a goal and reach it.

You can reach a stranger's heart with a smile or a kindness.

You can "reach for the stars."

REACH IT

FIX IT

I heard a story of a man who walked through every room in his house. He carried a pencil and paper with him. He wrote down every single thing he saw that needed fixing. He found over 200 things!

He got busy. He said that over a period of two years, he fixed nearly all of them.

Some people make a living by fixing things for others:

Fixing cars

Appliances

Bicycles

Computers

The list is almost endless.

Some people buy or collect things, fix or remodel them and sell them for a profit, like houses or watches.

Some people fix things as a hobby.

Some fix things to make their homes or neighborhoods nicer places to live.

Some fix things to help the elderly or those in need.

What can you find that you can fix?

FIX IT

COOK IT

Whenever I think of cooking, a story from my past comes to mind.

Some good friends of ours who used to live across the street from our family, moved to another city. I had been a babysitter for their two young children. Their mother, Jackie, was a fabulous cook.

A few years after they moved, they called me, and asked if I would come for a week to take care of their children while they (the parents) went on a trip. And Jackie wanted me to come a week early so she could teach me how to cook! Let me tell you, this was an adventure.

I had never done much cooking, baking yes, lots of cookies, but never cooking. Jackie taught me, but I'm not sure how much learning took place.

All I remember and all that they still remind me of to this day is that I cut the string off the rump roast before I cooked it.

If you have an opportunity to learn to cook, I strongly encourage you to do so.

COOK IT

PLAY IT

What games and sports do you enjoy playing?

These are some that I remember playing:

Monopoly

Scrabble

Chinese checkers

Checkers

Jacks

Hopscotch

Parcheesi

Canasta

Samba

Poker

Solitaire

Double Solitaire

Musical chairs

Swinging on swings

Sliding down slides

Boating

Playing in the sandbox

Playing with dolls and dollhouses

Playing with train sets

Hide and Seek

Croquet

Catch

Baseball

Ice skating

Ring around the Rosie

Charades

Swimming

Blind Man's Bluff

Walking

Hiking

Square Dancing

Tricycle riding

Bike riding

Jumping rope

Roller skating

Cheerleading

Miniature golf

Pool

Ping pong (my favorite)

Children of all ages, what games did you play or do you play?

PLAY IT

SEE IT

Right now where I am sitting, I can see on this November day:

evergreen trees, a gentle breeze blowing their branches

blue sky with a few white clouds

two birds that just lighted on a nearby rooftop

a peach tree that has lost all its leaves

an apple tree next to it with its green dry leaves still clinging to it

our garden, now bare dirt except for one delightful surprise – tiny lettuce leaves that just burst through the ground. They love the cool weather and had refused to appear during the heat of the summer.

a bird's nest (probably vacant now) clinging to some branches high up in a tree our flower garden that thanks to my husband's faithful cool weather watering still gave us two tiny bouquets on this day just 10 days shy of December

and mountain spires reaching to the sky in the distance.

What a day God has given!

SEE IT

WATCH IT

Do you ever enjoy just watching? It can be a peaceful, relaxing pastime.

Watching the sky at night, the moon, the stars.

Sometimes I see the Big Dipper or the Little Dipper.

Watching an airplane in the sky.

Sometimes where we live I can see in the distance a big jet climbing higher and higher on our side of the mountain and then, I can see it flying north for several minutes just above the top ridge of the mountain. I watch and watch as it flies until I can no longer see it.

Watching a butterfly as it flies through the air, rests on a flower, then glides up near a tree, up and down, back and forth, so daintily, so prettily, so gracefully.

Watching a kitten

jumping, running, rolling over, sleeping.

WATCH IT

INVENT IT

Here is a unique experience that I had when I was about ten years old.

At our church there was a little chapel. This was connected to the big church by another very small chapel.

At the back and up high in the big church was the choir loft with the big pipe organ.

In the back of the little chapel there was a pump organ. That meant that to get sound or music out of it a person had to be strong enough to pump that organ with his or her feet. My father was strong enough to play that pump organ and he played it every Sunday afternoon at the four o'clock service.

But my little grandmother, our church's main organist, could not pump the pump organ. Occasionally someone wanted to have a wedding in the little chapel on a weekday when my father was at work.

So this is what we did. My grandmother would sit at the organ in the choir loft of the big empty church.

Monsignor and the couple to be married would stand near the altar of the little chapel.

I would be stationed in the tiny middle chapel. I would watch Monsignor and when it was time to start the wedding march, he would give me a sign and I would run to the other end of the tiny chapel and wave my arms. My grandmother at the big pipe organ was watching for my signal and she would begin playing the wedding march. Whenever it was time for music during those weddings, we would follow this procedure. As far as I know it always went smoothly.

If you need a solution to a challenging situation, see if you can

INVENT IT

CHOOSE IT

In the early 1980s I lived in Oklahoma City. I could not teach piano at the place where I lived. An elderly chiropractor friend told me that during the depression (before he was a chiropractor) he knocked on doors to find work, roofing or whatever work he could find. He suggested that I try knocking on doors to find piano students and then go to their homes to teach them.

I chose to take his advice. I spent one summer, every evening and weekend, knocking on doors. I had the time of my life. People were so kind when I told them that I was a piano teacher. I met many women who had pianos but had never taken lessons until I knocked on their doors. My oldest student at that time was 79. She was a wonderful student. She practiced earnestly and made fine progress.

By knocking on doors I got all of my students, adults and children, within two or three miles, and I made many friends. Over the years I taught in more than 75 homes there.

In the 1990s when I moved to the Denver area I met my husband, Bill Mercer, and again I knocked on doors. I can remember now seventeen homes that I walked to and where I taught when I first moved there. When I knocked on one of those doors, a man opened the door and when I told him I was looking for piano students, he said "Come right in. I've got one for you." I taught his wife and she is still one of my best friends.

At one home a little boy was up in a tree near the sidewalk. When I told him what I was doing, he climbed down and went in to tell his mother. I taught him for several years.

My love of nature and my desire for fresher air often drew us to Evergreen, Colorado, in the mountains west of Denver. We eventually moved there and I again began knocking on doors. I built a large piano teaching business in Evergreen both by knocking on doors and thanks to the Canyon Courier, Evergreen's newspaper.

I have always let recitals be optional. I believe that some people thrive on competition and others do not. I have always given a lot of encouragement, and it was very rewarding when a child, after a year or so of lessons, chose to have a recital. He or she would have the recital in their home. This was a lot of work for the child. At most recitals, there are many children each playing one piece. When one of my students chose to have a recital, he or she would have to learn enough pieces to play for fifteen or twenty minutes. They invited their family and friends, printed up their own programs, and had a little party afterwards.

At one home I taught the mother and four children. Every year they had a family recital in their home. The father, an excellent pianist, also played in the recital.

One of my most special memories was a little girl I once taught who was so shy that she didn't even look at me during her lessons for the first several weeks. After a couple years she actually chose to give her own recital.

I met many of my dearest friends years ago when I knocked on their doors.

I owe my old chiropractor friend (now in Heaven) an eternal debt of gratitude for his suggestion to knock on doors to find students.

If someone offers you a suggestion that could change your life

CHOOSE IT

ADVERTISE IT

My husband, Bill, and I had many adventures during the years that we lived in a little cottage near Evergreen Lake in Evergreen, Colorado. This is one of them.

One day we taped a poster advertising my piano teaching business to a window facing the street.

The next morning we heard a noise outside the window. When we opened the blinds we saw a huge elk with its nose against the glass seemingly reading my ad. Bill said" "It pays to advertise, but where are you going to find a keyboard for those hooves?"

ADVERTISE IT

READ IT

I believe that my husband, Bill, was born reading. Whenever he isn't consciously doing some other task, he has a book in his hand. Reading for him is an interesting, relaxing pastime.

I love it when he tells me this story. When he was about nine years old, he went with his family on a camping trip. When it was time to go to bed he was just at the climax of the book he was reading. The campgrounds had a library. Bill had borrowed a book from the library and he had to finish it by morning because they were leaving. The rest of his family were asleep in their tents. The campground had some lamp posts. Bill got up, pulled a camp chair up to the base of the light pole and was reading when his father stepped from the tent, around two or three am, and spotted him. He was ordered back to bed but he finished his book at breakfast.

One time as a boy on the family farm in Michigan, Bill was sitting near a living room picture window reading. The sheep had gotten loose and his father and mother were outside running after them and calling to Bill to come and help. He was completely oblivious to their calls and their plight. His mother came up on the porch, stood outside the window where he was reading and called to him. Still he did not hear her. It wasn't until she came in and put her hand on his shoulder that he looked up. She said, "We need help". Bill said "oh ok" and went out to help them.

If you want to be industriously occupied every moment like Bill

READ IT

SNEAK IT

By my husband, Bill Mercer

My grandmother was a very talented baker. She made cakes and pies that inspired odes. However, one of the best things she made was homemade bread. I can still remember that heavenly aroma coming from the kitchen. The one thing that was frustrating to my father and myself was she insisted on the bread being cool before she would allow us to eat it.

One day my father and I devised a plan. Our home was designed such that there was both a front door and back door with access into the kitchen. The first step in this plan was that I would leave the house by the front door and run around to the back. At the appropriate time my father walked into the kitchen, took a bread knife from a drawer, and headed toward the loaves of bread which were cooling. My grandmother stopped him and scolded him for even thinking about eating hot bread. He loudly started to argue with her. This was my signal to sneak in the back door, scoop up a loaf of bread and some butter and sneak out the door again. As soon as my father saw this, he gave up his argument and went out through the front door to cool his temper. I joined him there.

With the bread knife which he had retained, he sliced several slices of the hot bread, lathered them with butter, and we proceeded with our feast. I suppose it wasn't the correct thing to do, and we got quite a lecture from my grandmother. However, I don't know when I enjoyed her bread more.

Sometimes you just have to

SNEAK IT

RELAX IT

By Bill Mercer

I remember a time as a teenager. Some friends of mine had formed a rock and roll band and were performing at the county fair. It was a "Battle of the Bands" competition, and I wanted to see how my friends would do. As usual we went to the fair as a family unit including my grandmother. We all went to a covered bleachers area which faced a stage on the other side of a horse racing track. Not knowing exactly when my friends would perform, we sat through two or three other band performances before my friends came on.

The wooden bleachers we sat on were shaking from the intensity of the sound. You could feel the reverberations from every group. We had been there some time before my friends came on, and I noticed my grandmother was getting tired. I promised we would leave as soon as they finished. Finally they were on. I don't know if they were the best but they were certainly the loudest of the afternoon. I paid strict attention to their efforts. At the conclusion, I turned around to see what my parents and grandmother thought. My grandmother was sitting upright with her mouth slightly open. However, it wasn't in awe. She had simply dropped off to sleep while sitting up, the bleachers shaking, and the loudest music of the day being played. I guess to her it was a lullabye.

RELAX IT

FOCUS ON IT

By Bill Mercer

When I was a freshman in high school, I played on a football team which had not had a winning record in many years. I went to a small school and it was sometimes difficult to find enough players. However, out of a freshman class of 45 students we fielded 12 players. I believe this was the first class which could put a full team on the field. We were in a six team league and also played three teams not in the league. Three of my classmates started for the varsity at quarterback, running back, and middle linebacker.

After the three non-league games we were 0 wins and 3 losses. Everyone suspected a long season. However, when the league season started, we began to win and after four games we were 3 wins, 3 losses, and 1 tie for the season. Our final game would be for the league championship.

The team we were to play had just joined our league that year. Their school was about twice the size of ours and had beaten every other team in the league by large margins. We weren't given much of a chance by the local newspapers, radio prognosticators, or even our own townspeople.

Our coach, who was also in his first year, found a tape by Pete Elliott who had been a head coach at the University of Illinois. The tape talked about many players who rose to great heights even though they were not his most gifted players. They simply believed they could do whatever it took.

He told of a game in which Illinois played against the University of Wisconsin with their All-American fullback Alan "The Horse" Ameche, one of the greatest players in football. The game was close, but Wisconsin began to wear down his team and moved the ball downfield. Wisconsin was about to score the winning touchdown and went into the huddle to call the play. At this point one of the Illinois linebackers yelled at the Wisconsin huddle "Hey Johnson, send Ameche at me!" This linebacker weighed about 170 pounds and Alan Ameche was well over 200 pounds. Pete Elliott said he was thinking what to write to the boy's mother after Ameche crushed him. However, when the play started, the Illinois backer rushed through the line, lifted Ameche off the ground, and put him on his back.

To this day when things look bad, I remember "Send Ameche at me!"

This tape had a profound effect on all of us. Our team became very focused on the task at hand. Practices all through the week were very intense. Finally Friday night arrived. Players began to arrive for the game as usual, but there was a difference. There was no talking, laughing, or joking around. Everyone came in, dressed in silence, and then went into the gym to relax before we took the field.

There was electricity in the air, but out of 25 – 30 boys of high school age there was no talking. Everyone was focusing on what he might be called upon to do. When we took the field our pre-game exercises were done crisply and with precision. When the game started, our blocking and tackling were the sharpest and hardest they had been all season. The intensity was like nothing I have experienced before or since.

We were smaller, probably slower, and less experienced, but we won the game 7 – 6. Our little town exploded in celebration. They formed a booster's club, graded and resurfaced the football field, built new dugouts for the baseball field, and purchased training equipment such as a hot tub and supplies.

The athletic program brought pride to the town. In the following years the school band won top honors in state competitions, the football team had undefeated seasons, the basketball team had several undefeated seasons, and the town itself took on a new attitude. They all found out what you can do if you

FOCUS ON IT

NOTICE IT

By Bill Mercer

Many years ago I was helping to coach a baseball team of boys aged six to eight years. Boys at that age tend to have a very short attention span as demonstrated by one of our young outfielders. He became absorbed in watching a butterfly flitting about him. The batter hit a ball that rolled between his legs. He was entirely oblivious to the fact and continued studying the butterfly. It took several seconds of yelling from us coaches, the parents in attendance, and some of his teammates before he realized that something had happened and located the ball. Therefore, we coaches were constantly yelling just to get someone's attention. One of the younger players was particularly frustrating. He was larger than the other boys his age, seemed to be more athletic than many of the others, and could have been one of the better players. However, he just didn't seem to care. This went on for several weeks. One game day I happened to see him arrive for the game. His parents drove up, let him out of the car, and drove away. I wondered if the reason he wasn't interested was because nobody seemed interested in him. I decided to try an experiment. Before the game I was hitting ground balls to a group of players. They were in a line and each took a turn at fielding the ball. The boy was one of the players in the line. When his turn came he made very little effort, but the ball bounced up and hit his leg. In the past I would have chided him for his lack of effort, but this time I said "Way to go, nice stop!" He looked at me strangely, but walked back to his place in line. When his next turn came he made an effort, but the ball bounced past him. This time I said "Nice try! That was a bad hop." The rest of the season I made an effort to praise anything he did, and we all began to see a steady improvement. My son and the son of the head coach were graduating from this age group, and we moved up with them. However, the third coach was the father of one of the younger boys, and he was going to coach them the following year. He said, "I don't know what I'm going to do with Tommy next year." The head coach and I looked at each other and said, "He may surprise you."

The following spring as I arrived for my son's practice, I noticed our team from the previous year at an adjoining field. As I took a second to watch them, I saw a ball hit toward Tommy. He moved to his right, reached across his body with his glove, backhanded the ball, straightened up and threw the ball on a line to the first base. I saw his coach and he told me Tommy was his best player. I hadn't done anything to make him a better player but encourage him. I was very happy I noticed his problem, and could give him what he needed.

NOTICE IT

CHERISH IT

By Bill Mercer

My mother was an extraordinary woman. She came from a large family with twelve children. As the oldest child she had to quit school in the eighth grade to help her mother and father. She worked very hard helping my grandfather on the farm and my grandmother in the house. She learned to cook for a large family on a limited budget, and learned to grow and harvest a large garden as well as helping my grandfather bring in the crops. After marrying my father, she continued handling many farm duties such as feeding the animals and growing a huge garden.

She planted fruit trees, had a good size strawberry patch, had a row of raspberry bushes, and grew tomatoes, peas, string beans, potatoes and many other vegetables.

She also knew the right time of year to harvest wild crops such as wild black raspberries, blackberries, morel mushrooms and hickory nuts. She canned and froze many of these things, and I remember spending a great deal of time with her harvesting the crops, roaming through the woodlands and pastures for the wild crops, and helping her with work on the farm.

She was also a fantastic cook who could make a great meal out of what many people would throw away. I still remember her baking powder bisquits with chicken gravy and giblets.

For all of the hard work, she was one of the most gentle, caring and soft spoken ladies you would ever hope to meet. She also loved doing craft projects, had a large number of house plants, sang in the church choir, participated in the Country Women's Improvement Club (CWIC), and later doted on her grandchildren.

Even though she had very little schooling, she was very perceptive and intelligent and took interest in a number of topics. Without being loud and obtrusive, she had the respect of everyone around her. She conducted her life with dignity even though no task seemed beneath her. I learned from her that no job is too small to be beneath your best effort. I miss her every day, but in many ways she will always be with me. I hope I have honored her memory by being the son she would want me to be.

CHERISH IT

QUOTE IT

My mother, Katherine Gedden, has been in Heaven for a little over a year now. Almost every day this past year something that she quoted or said to me during her life has come back to me. I wrote many of these down when they came to mind. She had heard many of them from her mother and her grandmother.

Some were old sayings. Others I have never read or heard anyone say but my mother.

I'd like to share these gifts from my Mom with you.

SAYINGS THAT I HEARD MY MOTHER SAY

"Where there's a will there's a way."

"That's the spirit."

"Look who's talking."

"First things first."

"It's better to be safe than sorry."

"Haste makes waste."

"Variety is the spice of life."

"So far so good."

"Live and let live."

"Here today, gone tomorrow."

"It'll either kill you or cure you."

"Don't rest on your laurels."

"Wet your whistle."

"Out of sight. Out of mind."

"A dime a dozen."

"Seize the moment."

"Sink or swim."

"Easy does it."

"You're barking up the wrong tree."

"We need to be on the same page."

"You can't get blood out of a turnip."

"A friend in need is a friend indeed."

"All work and no play makes Jack a dull boy."

"Don't count your chickens until they're hatched."

"Not in the least."

"Get a bang out of it."

"To each his own."

"More power to you."

"Tend to your knitting."

"Jack always said 'please'."

"A miss is as good as a mile."

"Don't cross your bridges until you come to them."

"Of all the nerve."

"You made your bed. Now lie in it."

"Don't rock the boat."

"An apple a day keeps the doctor away."

"Sticks and stones may break my bones, but words can never hurt me."

"Double your money."

"There are tricks to every trade."

"Don't mention it."

"Better late than never."

"For keeps."

"For the duration."

"In dire straits."

"The straw that broke the camel's back."

"You've got a lot on your plate."

"All in due time."

"What is right for the goose isn't right for the gander."

"You can't take it with you."

"Make hay while the sun shines."

"So much for that."

"Let your conscience be your guide."

"You can lead a horse to water but you can't make it drink."

"It's a piece of cake."

"There's a method to my madness."

"If the shoe fits, wear it."

"Last dibs."

"Mind your ps and qs."

"No news is good news."

"Never judge things by their appearance."

"It's all in the way you look at it."

"Let bygones be bygones."

"Practice what you preach."

"Are you keeping something up your sleeve?"

"All's well that ends well."

"Keep on keeping on." (I think this was my mother's favorite, especially in her last years).

"A lick and a promise."

"Don't let the bedbugs bite."

"If at first you don't succeed, try, try again."

"You're way ahead of me."

"Has the cat got your tongue?"

"Time is the great healer."

"Don't cry over spilt milk."

"Early to bed and early to rise makes a man healthy, wealthy and wise." -Benjamin Franklin

"O what a difference a day makes."

"All this and Heaven too."

"This too shall pass."

"Time's a wastin'."

"You don't eat enough to keep a bird alive."

"A bare bones description."

"The more the merrier."

"Praise someone to the skies."

"Waste not. Want not."

"That is the acid test."

"Beyond the shadow of a doubt."

"You can't have your cake and eat it too."

"A watched pot never boils."

"Act in haste. Repent at leisure". Bill quoted.

"Keep up the good work."

SAYINGS I HEARD ONLY MY MOTHER SAY

"Are you working your fingers to the bone and then working the bone?"

"I feel like a new woman."

"If you insist."

"Give me strength."

"Don't wake the sick lady on the east side."

"What do you wish you were doing?"

"Carry on."

"The dishes will always be with us."

"You never know what the day will bring."

"There'll be houses when we're dead and gone."

"Happy day before your Birthday."

"It's saving the day."

"What is this world coming to?"

"Are congratulations in order?"

"Don't sleep your life away."

"Are you still among the living?"

"No one can tell the other guy."

"Life goes on."

"Whoever heard of such a thing."

"God never made a bad day." Nana

"I'm not keeping you up am I?"

"I worry to a point and that's it."

"Let's talk about summer."

"I just love to watch people work."

"God be with you and have a good day."

"If you can't laugh you might as well pack it up."

"What difference will it make a hundred years from
now?"

"Let it be."

"I'm in my glory."

"Like I've died and gone to Heaven."

"Tomorrow's another day."

"That's about enough of that stuff."

"You're ahead of the game."

"Get off your high horse."

"Are you in there?"

"Ouch burn."

"Toasty warm."

"Use your head." Dad

"It's been nice knowin' ya."

"You don't mind if I groan a bit do you?"

"Don't say I never did anything for you."

"You're on your own."

"You're too much."

"Rise and shine."

"Hit the hay." Dad

"Use your best judgment." Dad and Mom

"Keep your chin up."

"I've got your number."

"Have a little of your own medicine."

"You're a card."

"Get your bearings."

"If wishes were fishes, beggars would ride."

"Have you solved all the problems of the world?"

"It's only a material thing."

And whenever we asked Dad and Mom what they wanted for Christmas or for Birthdays, they always said: "Peace and quiet."

"I'm going to go lie down until this little bit of dark passes over." -Bill's grandmother

"Wonders never cease."

"I think I'll call it a day."

QUOTE IT

LAUGH IT

"If you can't laugh, you might as well pack it up."

My mother quoted these words to me often, even at the age of 92.

It is said that:

"Laughter is the best medicine."

"Laughter is good for the soul."

This is my husband Bill's special gift. He brings joy and laughter wherever he goes.

My Dad had, and my four brothers have, a terrific sense of humor. I never could get ahead of them, especially my brother, Steve.

Another of our mother's favorite sayings was:

"I'm not keeping you up, am I?" I could always get a laugh from my piano students, even the children, if I said that to them when they seemed a little sleepy during their lessons.

The best friends are ones we can laugh with.

To bring joy to the world

LAUGH IT

PRAY IT

When we pray, we connect ourselves with the Infinite Power of the universe.

What we sow, we reap. When we sow prayers for others, for our world, we reap tremendous blessings. When we sow prayers for peace, we reap tremendous peace for ourselves. I think if there is any one quality to be sought after, to be nurtured, to be treasured, it is a feeling of inner quietness, of serenity, of peace. The world can be stormy. We can strive to make our minds and souls a safe harbor.

"Be still, and know that 'I AM' God." -Psalm 46:10

When we pray prayers of gratitude, our hearts overflow with joy.

And when we pray or just feel adoration of that Infinite Power, we know that we are never alone.

PRAY IT

LIVE IT

TODAY

Live this day.

Enjoy this day.

Rejoice in this day.

Be grateful for this day.

"THIS is the day the Lord has made. We (I) will rejoice and be glad in it." -Psalm 118:24

"Give us THIS day." -Matthew 6:11

God's strength, wisdom, assistance in every way are given THIS day. Why? Because yesterday is past and tomorrow isn't here yet. There IS only TODAY.

Life is for living!

LIVE IT! TODAY!

Made in the USA
San Bernardino, CA
29 October 2018